How to Retire Wealthy & Healthy

Dr. Binoy Gupta

Ukiyoto Publishing

All global publishing rights are held by

Ukiyoto Publishing

Published in 2024

Content Copyright © Dr. Binoy Gupta

ISBN 9789362698155

All rights reserved.

No part of this publication may be reproduced, transmitted, or stored in a retrieval system, in any form by any means, electronic, mechanical, photocopying, recording or otherwise, without the prior permission of the publisher.

The moral rights of the author have been asserted.

This book is sold subject to the condition that it shall not by way of trade or otherwise, be lent, resold, hired out or otherwise circulated, without the publisher's prior consent, in any form of binding or cover other than that in which it is published.

www.ukiyoto.com

Introduction

Retirement is the ugliest word English in the language.

Ernest Hemingway

I joined the Indian Revenue Service in 1968 and served as a tax administrator for almost four decades. Four decades is rather a long journey. But I thoroughly enjoyed the journey. I kept on studying - acquiring several postgraduate degrees and diplomas in various fields and a doctorate in law from the prestigious Bombay University.

I loved travelling and travelled whenever an opportunity came my way. I took photographs and wrote articles. These were published in most of the important magazines and newspapers of India. I also wrote several books. I was also a guest lecturer in various classes in the Madras University. And I kept pets and plants. My hobbies kept me busy and insulated from the worries often caused by my duties.

After my retirement, I had more time to read and travel. It was on one of my holidays in Jomtien Beach, Thailand, about 5 km. from the famous Pattaya Beach, I met several people from different countries of Europe. They were in their 40s or 50s. And they thoroughly enjoyed life. They used to spend several of the coldest months in Jomtien Beach.
Some of them told me that they had a lot of money and they did not do any work and why should they. Some of them had opted for premature retirement. This gave me a new perspective about retirement.

I decided to write a book for retired people and those who are planning for early retirement. I have discussed several issues that would make life after retirement stress-free, comfortable and happy.

Binoy Gupta

Contents

Chapter 1 : Concept of Retirement	1
Chapter 2 : Age of Retirement	10
Chapter 3 : Will	13
Chapter 4 : Senior Citizen	20
Chapter 5 : Maintenance of Parents and Senior Citizens Act, 2007	31
Chapter 6 : Old Age Homes	51
Chapter 7 : Retiring Early	56
Chapter 8 : Financial Planning	61
Chapter 9 : Health Planning	66
Chapter 10 : From my Personal Experiences	72
About the Author	74

Chapter 1 : Concept of Retirement

Life begins at retirement...
Author Unknown

Concept of Retirement

Have you ever wondered why we have an age of retirement? Who fixed it? What are the reasons for the selection of any particular age? And why should *you* not choose *your* own time of retirement?

History

To get to the root of the issue, let us look past the neighbouring Asian countries all the way to the beautiful sandy islands of Okinawa, Japan. According to the Okinawa Centenarian Study, men and women in Okinawa live an average of seven years longer than Americans and have one of the longest disability-free life expectancies in the world.

Dan Buettner and fellow researchers from National Geographic studied why Okinawans live so long. What did they find out? Among other things, Okinawans eat off of smaller plates, stop eating when they're 80% full, and have a beautiful setup wherein they're put into social groups as babies to slowly grow old together.

But they also have an outlook on life that is very different from those in the West. While we think of retirement as the golden age of golf greens and cottage docks, guess what they call retirement in Okinawa? They don't even think of retirement. They don't even have a word for it. Literally, nothing in their language describes the concept of stopping work completely. Instead, one of the healthiest societies in the world has the word ikigai (pronounced like "icky guy"), which roughly translates to "the reason you wake up in the morning." It's the thing that drives you most.

Toshimasa Sone and his colleagues at the Tohoku University Graduate School of Medicine wondered whether having an ikigai could actually help extend longevity, health, and late-life stability, so they put the concept to a test. They spent seven years in Sendai, Japan, studying the longevity of more than 43,000 Japanese adults with regard to age, gender, education, body mass index, cigarette use, alcohol consumption, exercise, employment, perceived stress, history of disease, and even subjects' self-rated scores of how healthy they were.

Then they asked every single one of these 43,000 people, "Do you have an ikigai in your life?" Participants reporting an ikigai at the beginning of the study were more likely to be married, educated, and employed. They had higher levels of self-rated health and lower levels of stress. At the end of the seven-year study, 95% of the folks with an ikigai were alive. Only 83% of those without an ikigai made it that long.

To put it another way: We don't actually want to retire and do nothing. We just want to do something we love. And I'm not talking about endless days of fishing and sailing off into the sunset. While we might want some time to do those things, you'd be surprised to learn how quickly the bloom can come off of that type of rosy retirement.

I believe that we'd all be better served by taking the concept of ikigai and distilling it into what I call the 4 S's:

1. Social: Friends, peers, and co-workers who brighten our days and fulfill our social needs.

2. Structure: The alarm clock ringing because you have a reason to get up in the morning, and the resulting satisfaction you get from earned time off.

3. Stimulation: Keeping our minds challenged by learning something new each day.

4. Story: Being part of something bigger than ourselves by joining a group whose high-level purpose is something you couldn't accomplish on your own.

Let us move over to Brazil, a country known for its vibrant and lively culture. In Brazil, retirement is seen as an opportunity for celebration and joy. Retirees in Brazil often engage in social activities and join community organizations creating a strong sense of camaraderie and belonging. The Brazilian government also offers a range of programs and incentives to encourage active ageing, promoting physical and mental well-being among retirees. With its lively music, colourful festivals, and zest for life, retirement in Brazil is a time for happiness and embracing the joys of the moment.

Concept of Retirement

The concept of retirement at a particular age is relatively new. Traditionally, most people worked till death, or till they became physically incapable of working any longer.

As our societies became more and more complex - guilds, or organizations comprising of craftsmen and merchants, grew up. The earliest guilds were formed in Europe during the 16th century. These guilds regulated production and employment. In times of poverty, illness, death and other emergencies, they also provided a range of benefits, including financial help, to their members.

Introduction of the Age of Retirement (Germany)

In 1889, Otto von Bismarck, the "Iron Chancellor" of Germany, introduced the world's first social security scheme to attract the German working class and counter the power of the Socialist Party in Germany.

Otto von Bismarck arbitrarily picked the age of retirement as 70. There was no rhyme or reason for his selection. But this was an extremely wise move. The program did not really cost the Government anything, because in those days, most German workers never lived to the age of even 65.

Some writers have erroneously written that U.S. adopted the age of 65 as the age for its retirement benefits based on Bismarck's selection of the age of 65 years, which he (Bismarck) had selected because he was 65 years old at the time of the selection.

But Bismarck was actually 74 at the time of selection of the age of retirement and he had actually selected the retirement age of 70 (and not 65 years). Only in 1916 (27 years after the selection by Bismarck), Germany lowered the age of retirement to 65. By this time, Bismarck had been dead for 18 years.

Social Security Act of 1935 (U.S.)

In the U.S., President Franklin D. Roosevelt enacted the Social Security Act on 14 August 1935 (55 years after Otto von Bismarck, the German Chancellor, had introduced it in Germany), to meet the economic problems caused by the Great Depression.

This Act provided that benefits were to be paid to a worker when he retired at the age of 65. The benefits to be paid were based on payroll contributions the worker made before retirement. But in those days, the average life expectancy in the U.S. was only 61.7 years.

The amendments to the Social Security Act in 1939 made a fundamental change in the Social Security program. The Amendments added two new categories of benefits:

1. Payments to the spouse and minor children of a retired worker (so-called dependents benefits); and

2. Survivor's benefits paid to the family in the event of the premature death of a covered worker.
This change transformed Social Security from a retirement program for workers into a family-based economic security program.

Social Security Amendments of 1961 (U.S.)

In 1956, women were given the option to retire early. But men became eligible for early retirement only in 1961 - after another 5 years. The amendments made to the Social Security Act in 1961 allowed workers to opt for reduced retirement benefits with early retirement at the age of 62. Workers could choose to retire at the full retirement age of 65 and receive full benefits.

Social Security Reform of 1980s (U.S.)

The Social Security crisis of the 1980s warranted further changes to the system. At present, experts recommend raising the retirement age to 70. They have calculated that this would save 95 cents of every dollar now spent on people 65 to 69 years old who have retired with full Social Security benefits.

Social Security in U.K. (The Poor Laws of U.K.)

British social policy was dominated by the Poor Laws, first passed in 1598 and continuing till 1948. The Elizabethan Poor Law of 1601 provided for:

1. A compulsory poor rate.
2. The creation of 'overseers' of relief.
3. Provision for 'setting the poor on work'.

The Parish was the basic unit of administration. There was no general mechanism through which this could be enforced, and the operation of the Poor Laws was quite different between different areas.

The changes due to the industrial revolution led to the development of the towns, rapid population growth, the first experiences of modern unemployment and the effects of the trade cycle. All this caused increasing poor rates.

The Poor Law Commission of 1834 emphasized two principles:
1. Less eligibility - the position of the pauper must be 'less eligible' than that of the labourer.
2. The workhouse test - no relief outside the workhouse.

The Poor Laws were much hated and despised, and much of the development of social services in the 20th century - including national insurance, means tests and health care - were framed to avoid having to rely on them.

The Welfare State in Britain (pre-1948)

William Beveridge, an Indian Civil Service officer, born in undivided India, can be considered the architect of the present Social Security System in the U.K.

Beveridge was invited to head a committee of officials to survey the then existing social insurance and allied services in the U.K., and to make recommendations for reforms. His Report to the Parliament on Social Insurance and Allied Services was published in 1942.
He proposed that all people of working age should pay a weekly national insurance contribution. In return, benefits would be paid to people who were sick, unemployed, retired or widowed.

Beveridge argued that this system would provide a minimum standard of living "below which no one should be allowed to fall". He recommended that the government should find ways of fighting the five 'Giant Evils' of:

1. Want,
2. Disease,
3. Ignorance,
4. Squalor and
5. Idleness.

Beveridge proposed a system of National Insurance, based on the following three fundamental 'assumptions':

1. Family allowances.
2. A National Health Service, and
3. Full employment.

(One of his three fundamental assumptions was that there would be a National Health Service of some sort, a policy which was already being worked upon in the Ministry of Health.)

Beveridge put forth his arguments in such a forceful and convincing manner that it became widely accepted. Beveridge appealed to Conservatives and other doubters by arguing that the welfare measures he proposed would increase the competitiveness of British industry in the post-war period, not only by shifting labour costs like healthcare and pensions out of corporate ledgers and onto the public account, but also by producing healthier, wealthier and thus more motivated and productive workers, who would also serve as a great source of demand for British goods. This became a major propaganda weapon, with both major parties committed to its introduction.

The Labour Government was elected in 1945. It introduced three key acts:

1. The 1946 National Insurance Act, which implemented the Beveridge scheme for social security;
2. The National Health Service Act 1946; and
3. The 1948 National Assistance Act, which abolished the Poor Law while making provision for welfare services.

These Acts were brought into force on the same day – on 7th June 1948. The 1948 Children Act was also brought into force on the same day.

The Welfare State in Britain (after 1948)

The key elements of a "Welfare State" were understood as encompassing:

1. Social Security
2. Health
3. Housing
4. Education and
5. Welfare and children (the 'personal social services').

The Poor Laws were enacted to help the poor. On the other hand, the Welfare Laws - the new measures of 1948 - were not for the poor. They were enacted to help everyone.

Retirement

Retirement at a particular age (which we will discuss in more detail in another chapter) was made possible by the old age pension given by employers or by the state.
Today, most developed countries have some sort of retirement benefit scheme. But in the poorer nations, the benefits are available only to a select few – to a few salaried employees and industrial workers. Most of the older generation have to be supported by the younger family members.

India

In India, even today, social security benefits are restricted to very few people, like government officials and those working in the organized sector.

There are a plethora of social welfare legislations like the Employees State Insurance Scheme, Provident Fund, etc. However, the benefits of these schemes are available to only a select few.

The Central Government, the State Governments and the public sector organizations have schemes for providing medical facilities (or reimbursement of medical expenses), provident funds and gratuity schemes for their employees. The medical facilities usually continue even after retirement.

But the age of retirement is neither uniform nor static. Even in India, it has changed over the years. The retirement age of Government of India officials was 55 years.

In December 1962, following the Chinese aggression, Prime Minister Jawaharlal Nehru found there were not enough personnel to run the ordinance factories. He issued a three-line order raising the retirement age from 55 to 58.

In 1998, the Government of India again raised the retirement age of its employees to 60 years. At present, there is a move to raise it to 62 years. After all, today people not only live longer, but also remain healthier.

The retirement age of Judges of the Supreme Court, High Courts and various other judicial and quasi-judicial posts varies between 65 and 70. The Law Commission of India has recommended that the retirement age of Chairpersons of all the Tribunals should be uniformly fixed at 70 years while the retirement age of Members of all the Tribunals should be fixed uniformly at 65 years.

On the other hand, for inexplicable reasons, the retirement age of employees of the Maharashtra Government employees is only 58 years.

Chapter 2 : Age of Retirement

> Retirement at sixty-five is ridiculous.
> When I was sixty five, I still had pimples.
>
> *George Burns*

Age of Retirement

The age of retirement is not the same everywhere. It differs from country to country. Even in the same country, it varies from time to time. It is often different for different categories of employees. For instance, there are different retirement ages for Central Government and State Government employees in India.

The age of retirement in different countries has changed over time due to a variety of factors:

1. Increasing life expectancy,
2. Availability, or shortage, of labour,
3. Trends in employment,
4. Personal attitudes to retirement, etc.

The Trend in the U.S.

The average age at which individuals retire has actually dropped continuously. In the U.S., it has dropped from 74 years in 1910 to 62 years in 2002. But at present, the trend is towards the opposite direction.

The reason is that in the coming years, the large bulk of the working-age population brought on by the early Baby Boom will begin to decline as Baby Boomers age and retire and the U.S. may experience a shortage of labour.

It is believed that businesses and the government will have so much need for workers that they will be obliged to offer special incentives, such as high pay, part-time work, and special benefits to prospective retirees, to entice them to remain at work for more years.

Should this come about, the days of incentives for early retirement may become a thing of the past. In their senior years, the seniors will continue to work for several more years, perhaps combined with more leisure time and activities.

The trend in Europe

Between 1995 and 2005, 16 European countries changed their retirement age. In practice, many people retire before reaching the normal retirement age, because of job loss, health or wealth conditions.

In most countries, early or premature retirement is allowed after a minimum number of working years. But this usually results in a proportionate reduction of the pensionary benefits.

Some people continue to work even after normal retirement. It is therefore quite common to find retired people working full-time or part-time while receiving pension income. But most such people usually work for lesser time and lesser pay. In this period of life, salary becomes a secondary consideration. They tend to look for more job satisfaction and a pleasant work environment.

Retirement in other Countries

As stated above, the retirement age varies from country to country. It generally varies between 55 and 70. In some countries, the retirement age is different for males and females (although in some countries, this has been challenged as discriminatory). In some cases, hazardous jobs carry a lower retirement age.

Retirement ceases if the retiree decides to go back to work. Typically, retirees who go back to work are people who find the lack of activity boring and work mainly for their own amusement, often turning a hobby into a job. Old-age pensions are usually not reduced because of other income, so the latter comes in addition to the former.

The Trend in India

In countries like India, most people have to work until they are physically capable of working. The Central Government, the State Governments, public sector organizations and the organized sector have retirement ages.

The age of retirement normally varies between 58 and 60 years. But there are post-retirement jobs where the retirement age increases up to 70 years. There is a move to increase the retirement age by various governments by a couple of years or so.

Concern of Government

The financial burden for providing pensionary benefits on the government's budget is quite heavy. Moreover, with an increase of longevity, the availability of new medical procedures which often involve quite a lot of money, the financial burden continues for a much longer period. And the burden goes on increasing year after year. This is the reason for political debate about the retirement age. At present, all Governments prefer a longer retirement age purely for economic considerations.

Chapter 3 : Will

A will is a legal document which lets a dead person do things which he could not do when he was alive.

Will

What is a Will

A will is a document made by a person (called a testator) during his lifetime. But it takes effect only after his death. It determines the manner, that is, to whom his property will go (devolve) after his death.

Section 2 (h) of the Indian Succession Act 1925 defines a "will" as: "...the legal declaration of the intention of a testator with respect to his property which he desires to be carried into effect after his death."

Is it necessary for a person to make a Will

No. It is not necessary for any person to make a will. But if a person dies without making a will, which in legal parlance is called intestate, his properties will automatically pass to his legal heirs, that is, according to the law of succession applicable to him.

If a person dies without making a will, his property will pass to his successors on the basis of the:

1. Hindu Succession Act 1956 (in the case of Hindus, Buddhists, Sikhs and Jains).
2. Mohammedan law of succession (in the case of Mohammedans) and
3. Indian Succession Act 1925 (in the case of others).

Let us say, I have three children – two sons and one daughter. My wife comes from a very rich family and has a lot of assets of her own. My daughter is married to a very wealthy family. My elder son is in the information technology sector. He is a multi-millionaire. My younger son is not doing well. Even then, he looks after me and his mother very well, trying to fulfill our every wish.

I would like to leave almost my entire estate, which consists of a good house, some jewellery and shares worth Rupees Ten lakhs to my younger son. If I die without making a will, all my properties will go to my wife and the three children in equal proportions.

If I make a will, I can give everything to my younger son; or to him and my wife in equal proportions, or in any other manner I like. Again, by means of a will, I can leave something to my faithful servant; and to my nurse who has taken very good care of me whenever I have fallen sick; and to a friend who has always helped me and is now in need of money (though he will never tell me this), and so on.

Must a Will be in Writing and Privileged Will

Under their personal law, Mohammedans can make an oral will. It need not be in writing. But in the case of all others - Hindus, Christians, Sikhs, Jews, Parsees, etc., the will has to be in writing.

The law provides some relaxation to soldiers and airmen employed in an expedition, or engaged in actual warfare; and to mariners at sea. These persons can make an oral will. Such a will is known as a *Privileged Will*.

Format of a Will

There is no specified or prescribed format of a will. It is not necessary to execute a will on stamp paper. A will can be made on a sheet of plain paper. However, since a will may be required after a long time, it is advisable to use good quality, durable paper.

You can write your will in your own handwriting, using a ball pen or an ink pen. But a handwritten will may create confusion and legal problems because of illegibility. It is therefore advisable to have the will typed in order to avoid any complications later. The language used in the will should be clear and unambiguous.

Legal documents generally have wide margins on both sides of the paper - because over the years, the paper often gets torn or mutilated at the edges.

Signing and attestation of a Will

Mohammedans (and members of the armed forces and mariners) can make an oral will. So there can be no question of signing it. But all others have to make a will in writing. The maker of the will also has to sign or affix his thumb impression on the will. (If he cannot do so, he can ask someone else to do so for him.)

Under 63 of the Indian Succession Act 1925:

(a) The testator shall sign or shall affix his mark (thumb impression) to the will; or it shall be signed by some other person in his presence and by his direction.

(b) The signature or mark of the testator, or the signature of the person signing for him, shall be so placed that it appears that it was intended thereby to give effect to the writing as a will.

(c) The will shall be attested by two or more witnesses, each of whom has seen the testator sign or affix his mark to the will or has seen some other person sign the will, in the presence and by the direction of the testator, or has received from the testator a personal acknowledgment of his signature or mark, or of the signature of such other person; and each of the witnesses shall sign the will in the presence of the testator. But it is not necessary that more than one witness should be present at the same time, and no particular form of attestation is necessary.
In simple language:

1. The person making the will should sign or put his thumb impression on the will - generally at the end.
2. If he is not capable of doing so (for instance, his hands are injured), he can ask some other person to sign or put his thumb impression on his (the testator's) behalf.
3. If there is more than one page in the will, he should sign each page at the end to avoid any possibility of tampering with the pages.
4. A will has to be attested by at least two witnesses. It is not necessary for all the witnesses to be present together. But each witness must actually see the testator sign or affix his thumb impression on the will, or receive an acknowledgment from him to this effect.
5. Each attesting witness must sign in the testator's presence.

In practice, the testator should call two witnesses, sign each page of the will, and then ask the witnesses to sign the will in his presence.

Alteration of a Will

Every correction, or alteration, in a will has to be signed by the testator. Any time after making the first will, a person can make a fresh will.
A person can also make a codicil - a document making some modifications to the original will. He should specifically refer to the original will in the codicil. The codicil is treated as part of the main will.

Selecting the Witnesses

You have to keep three important factors in mind while selecting the witnesses to your will.

1. They must have attained the age of majority.
2. The attesting witness and his (or her) spouse should not be a beneficiary under the terms of the will. In such an eventuality, the validity of other bequests under the will is not affected, but the bequest in favour of the witness and his/her spouse would become invalid.
3. Also ensure that they are not very old. Ideally, they should be a few years younger than you.

Registration of Will (Optional)

The law does not require registration of a will. Registration is purely optional. But if a will is registered, any changes can be made only through a registered deed.

How Wills are generally drafted

It is not necessary to use any formal, legal or technical language in drafting a will. A simple draft is given below.

The Will Format

A will has four main parts – Beginning, Recital, Operative part and the End.

The Beginning

A will normally begins like this: 'This is the last Will and testament of me, Shri ...., aged......years, son of ......, at present residing at ....

I hereby revoke all Wills and Codicils, if any, hereinbefore made by me and declare this to be my last Will. This will be operative after my death.'

The Recital

The beginning is followed by a recital which contains relevant background information. This part contains a list of the family members as well as details of the persons to whom the estate will pass.

This part also contains details of the various movable and immovable properties belonging to the testator which comprise his estate and which he intends to bequeath to his beneficiaries.

The Operative Part

This is the main part of the Will and contains details as to which property or portion thereof will go to whom. The testator may impose legally valid conditions on the beneficiaries.

For instance, he can put a condition that his son will get the properties only when he reaches the age of 25; or he will get the properties if he marries before a particular date. He can also allow his wife to live in a particular property during her lifetime.

The testator can name one or more persons to act as executors of the Will. I suggest you should name someone whom you trust.

The End

Some words, like the following, are usually added at the end of the will to show that all the legal requirements have been fulfilled. 'Signed by the within named testator Shri................., as his last Will and testament in our presence, all being present at the same time. Thereafter, at the request of the testator and in his presence and in the presence of one another, we subscribe our respective names.

Witnesses
Signature of testator

1. (Name, description and address)

2. (Name, description and address)

Helpful web site

You can find some useful information relating to wills at the following site:

https://www.mywealthguide.com/drafting-a-will

Chapter 4 : Senior Citizen

Uday Kotak who founded the Kotak Mahindra Bank nearly four decades ago, has been living a life of retirement since he stepped down as Chairman and Managing Director last September.

In his own words, he is enjoying the freedom of not being a regulated banker.

Senior Citizen

Senior Citizen is a dignified and respectable term for retired people. It is heartening that the Government of India has created a separate website for Senior Citizens listing out some of the special facilities available to them.

This is how the website starts:
Senior Citizens are a treasure in our society. They have worked hard all these years for the development of the nation as well as the community. They possess a vast experience in different walks of life. The youth of today can gain from the experience of the senior citizens in taking the nation to greater heights. At this age of their life, they need to be taken care of and made to feel special. Indian Government provides several benefits through its schemes in various sectors of development.
With various tax benefits, travel and health care facilities provisioned for them, Indian Government has created reasons for Senior Citizens to feel happy. This corner on Senior Citizens is aimed at providing details on various aspects concerning them.
The links pertaining to the following sections will take you to web pages/websites outside this website. For any query regarding the links of these websites/contents, please consult the web master of the respective website.

https://pensionersportal.gov.in/SeniorCitizenCorner.aspx#OldAge Homes

Nice, kind words. My sincere thanks to whoever scripted them.

Policies/Schemes

In 1999, the Government of India came out with the National Policy for Older Persons (NPOP) to promote the health and welfare of Senior Citizens in India. The main objective of this policy was to make older people fully independent citizens. This policy resulted in the launch of several new schemes for Senior Citizens. The policy defined a senior citizen as a person aged 60 years and above. Subsequent international efforts and declarations, such as the Madrid International Plan of Action on Ageing and the Political Declaration adopted by the UN General Assembly at the Second World Assembly on Ageing in April 2002, the Shanghai Plan of Action 2002, and the Macau Outcome Document 2007 adopted by UNESCAP, formed the basis of global policy guidelines to encourage governments to design and implement their own policies from time to time to suit their countries.

This had a serious impact on the implementation of our National Policy on Older Persons of 1999 because the Government of India is a signatory to all these documents. It tried its best to fulfill its commitment. New policies and plans were put in place by the central and state governments for the welfare of older persons. While some States and Union Territories implemented their policies with vigour, most states - particularly the big ones are lagging behind due to financial constraints and operational problems.

Pensions, travel concessions, income tax relief, medical benefits, extra interest on bank accounts, security of older persons, etc. were provided through an integrated scheme of the Ministry of Social Justice and Empowerment, as well as financial support for Old Homes, Day Care Centres, Medical Vans, Help Lines, etc.

Key Changes

1. The Government of India enacted the "Maintenance and Welfare of Parents and Senior Citizens Act, 2007 (commonly known as the Senior Citizens Act of 2007).
2. The Government of India Established the Department of Senior Citizens under the Ministry of Social Justice and Empowerment.
3. The Ministry of Social Justice and Empowerment established a "Department of Senior Citizens" which became the nodal agency for implementing programmes and services for senior citizens.
4. The 2011 National Policy for Senior Citizens (NPSC 2011) focuses on a number of issues, including an old age pension scheme that would cover all senior citizens living below the poverty line, with a monthly pension of Rs. 1,000 per person.
5. An inter-ministerial committee was formed to pursue matters relating to the implementation of the national policy and monitor its progress. Co-ordination is done by the nodal ministry. Each ministry prepares action plans to implement aspects that concern them and submit regular reviews.
6. States and union territories set up separate Directorates of Senior Citizens for implementing programmes and services for senior citizens and the NPSC 2011.
7. A National Commission for Senior Citizens at the centre and similar commissions at the state level were constituted. The Commissions were set up under the National Policy on Senior Citizens 2011 under an Act of Parliament with powers of Civil Courts to deal with cases pertaining to violations of rights of senior citizens.

The National Council for Senior Citizens is headed by the Minister for Social Justice and Empowerment with a tenure of five years to monitor the implementation of the policy and advise the government on the concerns of senior citizens. A similar body has been established in every state with the concerned minister heading the State Council for Senior Citizens.

Travel Benefits by Train

The Indian Railways used to give a substantial discount on their fares in all classes and in all trains - Sleeper Class, First Class, Air Conditioned (AC) Chair and First Class AC, in all trains, including Shatabdi and Rajdhani Expresses to Senior Citizens.
The minimum age for Senior Citizens for this particular concession was 60 years for males and 58 for females. The discount given was 40% for males and 50% for females.

Note: The senior citizens' concession was suspended in March 2020, because of the COVID-19 pandemic. Even though the pandemic-related shutdowns have all come to an end, this concession has not been restored.

The Railways also have special booking counters for senior citizens to prevent discomfort and health problems caused by standing in long queues. Of course, Senior Citizens also have the option of booking tickets through the online reservation system of Indian Railways: http://www.indianrail.gov.in

They can also book directly through the following site of the Indian Railway Catering and Tourism Corporation Ltd. (IRCTC): http://www.irctc.co.in

IRCTC charges Rs. 10 for sleeper class tickets and RS. 20 for all other tickets. The charge is levied on each transaction, irrespective of the number of tickets in that transaction.

Some trains, especially the local trains, have special coaches for Senior Citizens (and also for other handicapped persons) who use wheelchairs. These coaches have space for wheelchairs, handrails and a specially designed toilet. All major stations also have wheelchairs.

Old Age Homes (also called Old Homes)

Our modern lifestyle and fragmented families have necessitated Homes for the elderly. There are more than a thousand Old Age

Homes in India. Most of them offer free accommodation. Some Old Age Homes work on payment basis – their charges depending on the type of accommodation and quality of services offered.

Apart from food, shelter and medical amenities, Old Age Homes provide access to telephones and other forms of communication so that residents can keep in touch with their friends and relatives. Old Age Homes also provide reading material and recreational activities, such as, yoga classes. Some Old Age Homes have day care centres which take care of Senior Citizens only during the day.

Some states, such as Delhi, Kerala, Maharashtra and West Bengal have developed good quality Old Age Homes. These Old Age Homes have special medical facilities for Senior Citizens such as mobile health care systems, ambulances, nurses and provision of well-balanced meals.

For the older people who have no other place to go to, and no one to support them, Old Age Homes provide a safe haven. These Old Age Homes also provide a family-like atmosphere among the residents. Here, Senior Citizens find a sense of security, companionship and friendship. They can mix with people of their age group and share their joys and sorrows with them.

Under the Integrated Programme for Older Persons and other schemes, the Government of India is providing financial assistance of up to 100 % of the project cost to non-governmental organizations or NGOs for setting up Old Age Homes. The state governments are all providing similar financial assistance. The governments also provide liberal support to meet the day to day recurring expenses.

The financial assistance is given to establish and maintain old age homes, day care centres, mobile medicare units and to provide non-institutional services to older persons.

The Central Government Health Scheme

The Central Government Health Scheme provides total medical care to retired central government employees (pensioners). They can even obtain medicines for chronic ailments for up to three months at a time. The National Mental Health Programme focuses on the needs of senior citizens who are affected with Alzheimer's and other dementias, Parkinson's disease, depression and psycho-geriatric disorders. The State Governments and public sector undertakings also provide similar facilities.

Additional Interest on Bank Deposits

Senior Citizens enjoy additional benefits in investments in saving schemes and bank deposits. Almost all banks give Senior Citizens a slightly higher rate of interest than the rate given to the general public. Apart from these benefits, senior citizens also enjoy an annual interest rate of 9 percent on deposits made by them in post offices. They can open such an account in the nearest Post Office. This account can be transferred to any other post office throughout India.

In addition to the higher interest rates on deposits, senior citizens also enjoy exemptions from penalty for premature withdrawal of term deposits. When senior citizens encash their Fixed deposits (perhaps to tide over such emergencies such as sudden medical expenses and hospitalization), either they are exempted or charged a meagre percentage rate of their deposits.

Maintenance of Parents and Senior Citizens Act, 2007

This law requires earning adult children and grandchildren (excluding minors) to maintain and take care of their parents or grandparents. Maintenance refers to the provision of proper food, clothing, housing and medical treatment.
Parents (which includes biological, adoptive and step-parents) and any relative of a senior citizen who is in possession of property or who stands to inherit the property of the concerned senior citizen is liable

to provide maintenance under this Act. (I have reproduced this Act in Chapter 5 of this book for ready reference.)

An important feature of the law is that it provides protection not just to parents who are over the age of 60 years but also to every parent who is in need of care.

This law proposes the setting up of tribunals in every sub-division where aggrieved parents may complain about being neglected. All elders, who are unable to maintain themselves through their own earning or out of the property owned by them, are entitled to make an application to the Tribunal. The Tribunal will pass an order regarding the amount of maintenance to be provided. Children, grandchildren, or relatives may also face a jail term, have to pay a fine, or be disinherited from property bequeathed to them.

Age for availing benefits for senior citizens

Different sectors and organizations have prescribed different ages for offering discounts and benefits to senior citizens:

1. Banks and railways provide rebates, higher interests on deposits and other facilities to people above 60 years of age.

2. The Income Tax Department classifies a senior citizen as a person who is 65 years of age and above at any time during the relevant year.

3. Most airlines offer senior citizen discounts to males who are 65 years and above and females who are 63 years and above as on the date of commencement of the journey.

4. The minimum age of eligibility for old age pension varies from 55 to 65 years from state to state.

5. Senior Citizens Unit Plan of UTI offers the benefit of medical treatment to seniors and their spouses to those who are 58 years and older.

6. Unfortunately, the age for Senior Citizen benefits varies from 55 to 65 years depending upon the organization and the state concerned. The Government of India is trying to make it uniformly 60 years.

What a Senior Citizen should do to ensure safety

More and more children are leaving their parents for richer pastures in large cities or abroad. Senior Citizens, who are left alone, are comparatively more vulnerable to crime. The number of crimes against senior citizens is increasing.

They should take the following precautions to avoid them:

1. Register the names of their domestic help and drivers at the nearest police station by filling in the appropriate form. The police station will get their background verified.

2. Install safety features such as a CCTV, peephole facility, safety latch, or iron grill.

3. Should not open cupboards, display valuables, or discuss financial matters in front of their domestic help. This could tempt them to carry out an unlawful act.

4. Should not keep valuables at home. They should store jewellery in a bank locker and cash in their savings account. They should keep a dog, if possible.

5. Should not withhold pay, derogate, or mistreat domestic workers. This may provoke them to seek revenge.

6. Develop a network of friends and talk to their neighbours to ensure that they do not live a secluded life. They should go for regular walks in groups and socialize. This would help them keep happy and show that they have friends who are interested in their welfare.

7. Keep important telephone numbers handy. This includes lists of friends or relatives living nearby as well as that of the local police station, ambulance and other utilities.

Senior Citizen Reverse Mortgage Loan

A large part of the savings of Senior Citizens could be tied up in non-liquid assets like homes and property. Senior Citizens usually do not have a regular income and if they exhaust their savings, perhaps due to medical emergencies and the like, then it becomes difficult to meet living expenses without having to sell their house.

A Reverse Mortgage allows a Senior Citizen who owns a house to avail of a monthly stream of income against mortgage of the house. The Senior Citizen remains the owner and occupies the house throughout his or her lifetime, without repayment or servicing of the loan. This system allows Senior Citizens to convert their homes into cash without selling their property.

The amount a Senior Citizen may receive per month under the Reverse Mortgage is determined by the value of the property, the age of the Senior Citizen, and the prevalent interest rate. Generally, people who have a more valuable home and are older, get a larger amount of money per month. The monthly amount paid by the reverse mortgage company can be used to meet regular monthly expenses, medical expenses, etc. The borrower does not need to repay the loan as long as he/she continues to live in the house.

After the death of the Senior Citizen, the lending institution sells the house to recover the amount of the mortgage plus interest. All amounts in excess are given to the heirs of the borrower.

The basic difference between a reverse mortgage and a regular mortgage is the fact that a reverse mortgage has no predetermined tenure and does not have to be paid back in monthly installments. This makes it extremely useful for Senior Citizens.

You can get more details of the Reverse Mortgage system from the following website of the National Housing Board:

http://www.nhb.org.in

Senior Citizens Identity Card

Obtain this card to avail of the additional benefits and facilities.

Eligibility Criteria for Senior Citizenship Card

You must have an identity card and must be at least 60 years old.

Where to Apply for a Senior Citizenship Card

You have to apply for a Senior Citizenship Card on the state's official website of the state where you live.

You must complete the application form, attach all required documentation, and pay the registration price before submitting it. You can submit an application for the Senior Citizenship Card online or offline by going to the nearest facilitation centre (about which you can find out online).

Documents required for Senior Citizenship Card

Given below is the list of documents you usually need to submit to apply for a Senior Citizenship Card:

Identity Proof (Any one)

- Aadhaar Card
- Voter ID Card
- Passport
- Driving License
- Ration Card
- Pension Card
- Government issued photo identity card
- Bank certificate from the bank branch

Address Proof (Any one)
- Passport
- Telephone bill which should be generated in your name

- Aadhaar Card
- Ration Card
- Voter ID Card
- Rental Agreement
- Record of revenue
- Registered sale deed
- Passbook of your bank account with your photo
- Certified voter list

Age Proof (Any one)

- Birth certificate
- Passport
- PAN Card
- School Leaving Certificate

Benefits of having a Senior Citizenship Card

The following are some of the benefits of owning a Senior Citizenship card -
- Old-age home benefits can be availed of by Senior Citizens in case they are unable to sustain themselves financially.
- The validity of the card is throughout the country.
- Legal cases can be heard on priority.
- Discounts can be availed at government hospitals.
- Discounts are offered on bus tickets.
- Tax benefits can be availed.
- Banks offer higher interest rates.

Chapter 5: Maintenance of Parents and Senior Citizens Act, 2007

Retirement has been a discovery of beauty for me. I never had the time before to notice the beauty of my grand kids, my wife, the tree outside my very own front door. And, the beauty of time itself.

~Hartman Jule

Maintenance of Parents and Senior Citizens Act, 2007 (Senior Citizens Act and Rules)

There are cases where the children do not look after their old parents after retirement - especially when they stop earning. There are cases where the parents transfer everything they own to their children and the children just leave them to their fate.

In one case - India Today News Desk New Delhi, UPDATED: March 31, 2023
Jagdish Chandra Arya (78) and Bhagli Devi (77) were found dead in their home in Shiv Colony of Badhra in Charkhi Dadri, Haryana. The elderly couple committed suicide by consuming sulphas tablets on the night of March 29, 2023 leaving behind a suicide note accusing family members of atrocities. The couple said their son owns property worth Rs 30 crore but refused to feed them.

Another case - Vijaypat versus Gautam Singhania
It all started in 2015 when Vijaypat Singhania, the former chairman of Raymond Ltd, one of the largest makers of worsted suiting fabric in the world and a leader in India, transferred all his shares in Raymond, a 37.17% stake worth around Rs 1,000 crore at that time, to his son Gautam Singhania. He had to literally fight for a residence. Later, the tycoon of yesterday did not even have a car and a driver and lived in a

rented row house in Mumbai. I believe the issue has been recently sorted out.

The Maintenance of Parents and Senior Citizens Act, 2007 and Rules (commonly known the Senior Citizens Act and Rules), provide a framework that upholds the rights and protections of our seniors. The laws safeguard the rights of our seniors, ensuring that they are free from abuse, neglect, and exploitation. This protection is not merely a legal obligation; it is a moral imperative that resonates with the very essence of our collective humanity. And there is a simple machinery to enforce these rights. I am including the full text of the Act in this Chapter.

THE MAINTENANCE AND WELFARE OF PARENTS AND SENIOR CITIZENS ACT, 2007
ARRANGEMENT OF SECTIONS

CHAPTER I
PRELIMINARY

SECTIONS 1. Short title, extent, application and commencement.
1. Definitions.
2. Act to have overriding effect.

CHAPTER II
MAINTENANCE OF PARENTS AND SENIOR CITIZENS

1. Maintenance of parents and senior citizens.
2. Application for maintenance.
3. Jurisdiction and procedure.
4. Constitution of Maintenance Tribunal.
5. Summary procedure in case of inquiry.
6. Order for maintenance.
7. Alteration in allowance.
8. Enforcement of order of maintenance.
9. Option regarding maintenance in certain cases.
10. Deposit of maintenance amount.
11. Award of interest where any claim is allowed.
12. Constitution of Appellate Tribunal.
13. Appeals.
14. Right to legal representation.
15. Maintenance Officer.

CHAPTER III
ESTABLISHMENT OF OLD AGE HOMES

1. Establishment of old age homes.

CHAPTER IV

PROVISIONS FOR MEDICAL CARE OF SENIOR CITIZEN
1. Medical support for senior citizens.

CHAPTER V
PROTECTION OF LIFE AND PROPERTY OF SENIOR CITIZEN

1. Measures for publicity, awareness, etc., for welfare of senior citizens.
2. Authorities who may be specified for implementing the provisions of this Act.
3. Transfer of property to be void in certain circumstances.

CHAPTER VI
OFFENCES AND PROCEDURE FOR TRIAL
SECTIONS

1. Exposure and abandonment of senior citizen.
2. Cognizance of offences.

CHAPTER VII
MISCELLANEOUS

1. Officers to be public servants.
2. Jurisdiction of civil courts barred.
3. Protection of action taken in good faith.
4. Power to remove difficulties.
5. Power of Central Government to give directions.
6. Power of Central Government to review.
7. Power of State Government to make rules.

[*29 December*, 2007.]
An Act to provide for more effective provisions for the maintenance and welfare of parents and senior citizens guaranteed and recognised under the Constitution and for matters connected therewith or incidental thereto.

BE it enacted by Parliament in the Fifty-eighth Year of the Republic of India as follows:—

CHAPTER I
PRELIMINARY

1. Short title, extent, application and commencement.—

1. This Act may be called the Maintenance and Welfare of Parents and Senior Citizens Act, 2007.
2. It extends to the whole of India except the State of Jammu and Kashmir and it applies also it citizens of India outside India.
3. It shall come into force in a State on such date as the State Government may, by notification in the Official Gazette, appoint.

2. Definitions.—

In this Act, unless the context otherwise requires,—

a. "children" includes son, daughter, grandson and grand-daughter but does not include a minor;
b. "maintenance" includes provisions for food, clothing, residence and medical attendance and treatment;
c. "minor" means a person who, under the provisions of the Majority Act, 1875 (9 of 1875) is deemed not to have attained the age of majority;
d. "parent" means father or mother whether biological, adoptive or step father or step mother, as the case may be, whether or not the father or the mother is a senior citizen;
e. "prescribed" means prescribed by rules made by the State Government under this Act;

f. "property" means property of any kind, whether movable or immovable, ancestral or self-acquired, tangible or intangible and includes rights or interests in such property;

g. "relative" means any legal heir of the childless senior citizen who is not a minor and is in possession of or would inherit his property after his death;

h. "senior citizen" means any person being a citizen of India, who has attained the age of sixty years or above; "State Government",

i. relation to a Union territory, means the administrator thereof appointed under article 239 of the Constitution;

j."Tribunal" means the Maintenance Tribunal constituted under section 7; k."Welfare" means provision for food, health care, recreation centres and other amenities necessary for the senior citizens.

3. Act to have overriding effect.—

The provisions of this Act shall have effect notwithstanding anything inconsistent therewith contained in any enactment other than this Act, or in any instrument having effect by virtue of any enactment other than this Act.

CHAPTER II
MAINTAINANCE OF PARENTS AND SENIOR CITIZENS

4. Maintenance of parents and senior citizens.—

(*1*) A senior citizen including parent who is unable to maintain himself from his own earning or out of the property owned by him, shall be entitled to make an application under section 5 in case of—

i) parent or grand-parent, against one or more of his children not being a minor;

ii) a childless senior citizen, against such of his relative referred to in clause (*g*) of section 2.

(2) The obligation of the children or relative, as the case may be, to

maintain a senior citizen extends to the needs of such citizen so that senior citizen may lead a normal life.

(3) The obligation of the children to maintain his or her parent extends to the needs of such parent either father or mother or both, as the case may be, so that such parent may lead a normal life.

(4) Any person being a relative of a senior citizen and having sufficient means shall maintain such senior citizen provided he is in possession of the property of such citizen or he would inherit the property of such senior citizen:
Provided that where more than one relatives are entitled to inherit the property of a senior citizen, the maintenance shall be payable by such relative in the proportion in which they would inherit his property.

5. Application for maintenance.—

(1) An application for maintenance under section 4, may be made—
1. by a senior citizen or a parent, as the case may be; or
2. if he is incapable, by any other person or organisation authorised by him; or (c) the Tribunal may take cognizance *suo motu.*

Explanation.—For the purposes of this section "organisation" means any voluntary association registered under the Societies Registration Act, 1860 (21 of 1860) or any other law for the time being in force.

(2) The Tribunal may, during the pendency of the proceeding regarding monthly allowance for the maintenance under this section, order such children or relative to make a monthly allowance for the interim maintenance of such senior citizen including parent and to pay the same to such senior citizen including parent as the Tribunal may from time to time direct.

(3) On receipt of an application for maintenance under subsection (1), after giving notice of the application to the children or relative and after giving the parties an opportunity of being heard, hold an inquiry for determining the amount of maintenance.

(4) An application filed under sub-section (2) for the monthly allowance for the maintenance and expenses for proceeding shall be

disposed of within ninety days from the date of the service of notice of the application to such person: Provided that the Tribunal may extend the said period, once for a maximum period of thirty days in exceptional circumstances for reasons to be recorded in writing.

(5) An application for maintenance under sub-section (*1*) may be filled against one or more persons: Provided that such children or relative may implead the other person liable to maintain parent in the application for maintenance.

(6) Where a maintenance order was made against more than one person, the death of one of them does not affect the liability of others to continue paying maintenance.

(7) Any such allowance for the maintenance and expenses for proceeding shall be payable from the date of the order, or, if so ordered, from the date of the application for maintenance or expenses of proceeding, as the case may be.

(8) If, children or relative so ordered fail, without sufficient cause to comply with the order, any such Tribunal may, for every breach of the order, issue a warrant for levying the amount due in the manner provided for levying fines, and may sentence such person for the whole, or any part of each month's allowance for the maintenance and expenses of proceeding, as the case be, remaining unpaid after the execution of the warrant, to imprisonment for a term which may extend to one month or until payment if sooner made whichever is earlier:

Provided that no warrant shall be issued for the recovery of any amount due under this section unless application be made to the Tribunal to levy such amount within a period of three months from the date on which it became due.

6. Jurisdiction and procedure.—

(*1*) The proceedings under section 5 may be taken against any children or relative in any district—

(a) where he resides or last resided; or
(b) where children or relative resides.

(2) On receipt of the application under section 5, the Tribunal shall issues a process for procuring the presence of children or relative against whom the application is filed.

(3) For securing the attendance of children or relative the Tribunal shall have the power of a Judicial Magistrate of first class as provided under the Code of Criminal Procedure, 1973 (2 of 1974).

(4) All evidence to such proceedings shall be taken in the presence of the children or relative against whom an order for payment of maintenance is proposed to be made, and shall be recorded in the manner prescribed for summons cases: Provided that if the Tribunal is satisfied that the children or relative against whom an order for payment of maintenance is proposed to be made is wilfully avoiding service, or wilfully neglecting to attend the Tribunal, the Tribunal may proceed to hear and determine the case *ex parte*.

(5) Where the children or relative is residing out of India, the summons shall be served by the Tribunal through such authority, as the Central Government may by notification in the official Gazette, specify in this behalf.

(6) The Tribunal before hearing an application under section 5 may, refer the same to a Conciliation Officer and such Conciliation Officer shall submit his findings within one month and if amicable settlement has been arrived at, the Tribunal shall pass an order to that effect.

Explanation.—For the purposes of this sub-section "Conciliation Officer" means any person or representative of an organisation referred to in *Explanation* to sub-section (*1*) of section 5 or the Maintenance Officers designated by the State Government under sub-section (*1*) of section 18 or any other person nominated by the Tribunal for this purpose.

7. Constitution of Maintenance Tribunal.—

(*1*) The State Government shall within a period of six months from the date of the commencement of this Act, by notification in Official Gazette, constitute for each Sub-division one or more Tribunals as may be specified in the notification for the purpose of adjudicating and deciding upon the order for maintenance under section 5.

(2) The Tribunal shall be presided over by an officer not below the rank of Sub- Divisional Officer of a State.

(3) Where two or more Tribunals are constituted for any area, the State Government may, by general or special order, regulate the distribution of business among them.

8. Summary procedure in case of inquiry.—

(*1*) In holding any inquiry under section 5, the Tribunal may, subject to any rules that may be prescribed by the State Government in this behalf, follow such summary procedure as it deems fit.

(2) The Tribunal shall have all the powers of a Civil Court for the purpose of taking evidence on oath and of enforcing the attendance of witnesses and of compelling the discovery and production of documents and material objects and for such other purposes as may be prescribed; and the Tribunal shall be deemed to be a Civil Court for all the purposes of section 195 and Chapter XXVI of the Code of Criminal Procedure, 1973 (2 of 1974).

(3) Subject to any rule that may be made in this behalf, the Tribunal may, for the purpose of adjudicating and deciding upon any claim for maintenance, choose one or more persons possessing special knowledge of any matter relevant to the inquiry to assist it in holding the inquiry.

9. Order for maintenance.—

(*1*) If children or relatives, as the case may be, neglect or refuse to maintain a senior citizen being unable to maintain himself, the Tribunal may, on being satisfied of such neglect or refusal, order such children or relatives to make a monthly allowance at such monthly rate for the maintenance of such senior citizen, as the Tribunal may deem fit and to pay the same to such senior citizen as the Tribunal may, from time to time, direct.

(2) The maximum maintenance allowance which may be ordered by such Tribunal shall be such as may be prescribed by the State Government which shall not exceed ten thousand rupees per month.

10. Alteration in allowance.—

(1) On proof of misrepresentation or mistake of fact or a change in the circumstances of any person, receiving a monthly allowance under section 9, for the maintenance ordered under that section to pay a monthly allowance for the maintenance, the Tribunal may make such alteration, as it thinks fit, in the allowance for the maintenance.

(2) Where it appears to the Tribunal that, in consequence of any decision of a competent Civil Court, any order made under section 9 should be cancelled or varied, it shall cancel the order or, as the case may be, vary the same accordingly.

11. Enforcement of order of maintenance.—

(1) A copy of the order of maintenance and including the order regarding expenses of proceedings, as the case may be, shall be given without payment of any fee to the senior citizen or to parent, as the case may be, in whose favour it is made and such order may be enforced by any Tribunal in any place where the person against whom it is made, such Tribunal on being satisfied as to the identity of the parties and the non-payment of the allowance, or as the case may be, expenses, due.

(2) A maintenance order made under this Act shall have the same force and effect as an order passed under Chapter IX of the Code of Criminal Procedure, 1973 (2 of 1974) and shall be executed in the manner prescribed for the execution of such order by that Code.

12. Option regarding maintenance in certain cases.—

Notwithstanding anything contained in Chapter IX of the Code of Criminal Procedure 1973 (2 of 1974) where a senior citizen or a parent is entitled for maintenance under the said Chapter and also entitled for maintenance under this Act may, without prejudice to the provisions of Chapter IX of the said Code, claim such maintenance under either of those Acts but not under both.

Deposit of maintenance amount.—When an order is made under this Chapter, the children or relative who is required to pay any amount in terms of such order shall within thirty days of the date of announcing the order by the Tribunal, deposit the entire amount ordered in such manner as the Tribunal may direct.

13. Award of interest where any claim is allowed.—

Where any Tribunal makes an order for maintenance made under this Act, such Tribunal may direct that in addition to the amount of maintenance, simple interest shall also be paid at such rate and from such date not earlier than the date of making the application as may be determined by the Tribunal which shall not be less than five per cent. and not more than eighteen per cent.
Provided that where any application for maintenance under Chapter IX of the Code of Criminal Procedure, 1973 (2 of 1974) is pending before a Court at the commencement of this Act, then the Court shall allow the withdrawal of such application on the request of the parent and such parent shall be entitled to file an application for maintenance before the Tribunal.

14. Award of interest where any claim is allowed

Where any Tribunal makes an order for maintenance made under this Act, such Tribunal may direct that in addition to the amount of maintenance, simple interest shall also be paid at such rate and from such date not earlier than the date of making the application as may be determined by the Tribunal which shall not be less than five per cent, and not more than eighteen per cent:

Provided that where any application for maintenance under Chapter IX of the Code of Criminal Procedure, 1973 is pending before a Court at the commencement of this Act, then the Court shall allow the withdrawal of such application on the request of the parent and such parent shall be entitled to file an application for maintenance before the Tribunal.

15. Constitution of Appellate Tribunal.—

(1) The State Government may, by notification in the Official Gazette, constitute one Appellate Tribunal for each district to hear the appeal against the order of the Tribunal.

(2) The Appellate Tribunal shall be presided over by an officer not below the rank of District Magistrate.

16. Appeals.—

(1) Any senior citizen or a parent, as the case may be, aggrieved by an order of a Tribunal may, within sixty days from the date of the order, prefer an appeal to the Appellate Tribunal: Provided that on appeal, the children or relative who is required to pay any amount in terms of such maintenance order shall continue to pay to such parent the amount so ordered, in the manner directed by the Appellate Tribunal: Provided further that the Appellate Tribunal may, entertain the appeal after the expiry of the said period of sixty days, if it is satisfied that the appellant was prevented by sufficient cause from preferring the appeal in time.

(2) On receipt of an appeal, the Appellate Tribunal shall, cause a notice to be served upon the respondent.

(3) The Appellate Tribunal may call for the record of proceedings from the Tribunal against whose order the appeal is preferred.

(4) The Appellate Tribunal may, after examining the appeal and the records called for either allow or reject the appeal.

(5) The Appellate Tribunal shall, adjudicate and decide upon the appeal filed against the order of the Tribunal and the order of the Appellate Tribunal shall be final: Provided that no appeal shall be rejected unless an opportunity has been given to both the parties of being heard in person or through a dully authorised representative.

(6) The Appellate Tribunal shall make an endeavour to pronounce its order in writing within one month of the receipt of an appeal.

(7) A copy of every order made under sub-section (*5*) shall be sent to both the parties free of cost.

17. Right to legal representation.—

Notwithstanding anything contained in any law, no party to a proceeding before a Tribunal or Appellate Tribunal shall be represented by a legal practitioner.

18. Maintenance Officer.—

(*1*) The State Government shall designate the District Social Welfare or an officer not below the rank of a District Social Welfare Officer, by whatever name called as Maintenance Officer.

(*2*) The Maintenance Officer referred to in sub-section (*1*), shall represent a parent if he so desires, during the proceedings of the Tribunal, or the Appellate Tribunal, as the case may be.

CHAPTER III
ESTABLISHMENT OF OLD AGE HOMES

19. Establishment of old age homes.—

(*1*) The State Government may establish and maintain such number of old age homes at accessible places, as it may deem necessary, in a phased manner, beginning with at least one in each district to accommodate in such homes a minimum of one hundred fifty senior citizens who are indigent.

(*2*). The State Government may, prescribe a scheme for management of old age homes, including the standards and various types of services to be provided by them which are necessary for medical care and means of entertainment to the inhabitants of such homes.
Explanation.—For the purposes of this section, "indigent" means any senior citizen who is not having sufficient means, as determined by the State Government, from time to time, to maintain himself.

CHAPTER IV
PROVISIONS FOR MEDICAL CARE OF SENIOR CITIZEN

20. Medical support for senior citizens.—

The State Government shall ensure that,—

(i) the Government hospitals or hospitals funded fully or partially by the Government shall provide beds for all senior citizens as far as possible;
(ii) separate queues be arranged for senior citizens;
(iii) facility for treatment of chronic, terminal and degenerative diseases is expanded for senior citizens;
(iv) research activities for chronic elderly diseases and ageing expanded;

(v) there are earmarked facilities for geriatric patients in every district hospital dully headed by a medical officer with experience in geriatric care.

CHAPTER V
PROTECTION OF LIFE AND PROPERTY OF SENIOR CITIZEN

21. Measures for publicity, awareness, etc., for welfare of senior citizens.—

The State Government shall, take all measures to ensure that—

(i) the provisions of this Act are given wide publicity through public media including the television, radio and the print, at regular intervals;

(ii) the Central Government and State Government Officers, including the police officers and the members of the judicial service, are given periodic sensitization and awareness training on the issues relating to this Act;

(iii) effective co-ordination between the services provided by the concerned Ministries or Departments dealing with law, home affairs, health and welfare, to address the issues relating to the welfare of the senior citizens and periodical review of the same is conducted.

22. Authorities who may be specified for implementing the provisions of this Act.—

(*1*) The State Government may, confer such powers and impose such duties on a District Magistrate as may be necessary, to ensure that the provisions of this Act are properly carried out and the District Magistrate may specify the officer, subordinate to him, who shall exercise all or any of the powers, and perform all or any of the duties, so conferred or imposed and the local limits within which such powers or duties shall be carried out by the officer as may be prescribed.

(2) The State Government shall prescribe a comprehensive action plan for providing protection of life and property of senior citizens.

23. Transfer of property to be void in certain circumstances.—

(1) Where any senior citizen who, after the commencement of this Act, has transferred by way of gift or otherwise, his property, subject to the condition that the transferee shall provide the basic amenities and basic physical needs to the transferor and such transferee refuses or fails to provide such amenities and physical needs, the said transfer of property shall be deemed to have been made by fraud or coercion or under undue influence and shall at the option of the transferor be declared void by the Tribunal.

(2) Where any senior citizen has a right to receive maintenance out of an estate and such estate or part thereof is transferred, the right to receive maintenance may be enforced against the transferee if the transferee has notice of the right, or if the transfer is gratuitous; but not against the transferee for consideration and without notice of right.

(3) If, any senior citizen is incapable of enforcing the rights under sub-sections *(1)* and *(2)*, action may be taken on his behalf by any of the organisation referred to in *Explanation* to sub-section *(1)* of section 5.

CHAPTER VI
OFFENCES AND PROCEDURE FOR TRIAL

24. Exposure and abandonment of senior citizen.—
Whoever, having the care or protection of senior citizen leaves, such senior citizen in any place with the intention of wholly abandoning such senior citizen, shall be punishable with imprisonment of either description for a term which may extend to three months or fine which may extend to five thousands rupees or with both.

25. Cognizance of offences.—

(*1*)Notwithstanding anything contained in the Code of Criminal Procedure, 1973 (2 of 1974), every offence under this Act shall be cognizable and bailable.

(*2*) An offence under this Act shall be tried summarily by a Magistrate.

CHAPTER VII
MISCELLANEOUS

26. Officers to be public servants.—Every officer or staff appointed to exercise functions under this Act shall be deemed to be a public servant within the meaning of section 21 of the Indian Penal Code (45 of 1860).

27. Jurisdiction of civil courts barred.—No Civil Court shall have jurisdiction in respect of any matter to which any provision of this Act applies and no injunction shall be granted by any Civil Court in respect of anything which is done or intended to be done by or under this Act.

28. Protection of action taken in good faith.—No suit, prosecution or other legal proceeding shall lie against the Central Government, the State Governments or the local authority or any officer of the Government in respect of anything which is done in good faith or intended to be done in pursuance of this Act and any rules or orders made thereunder.

29. Power to remove difficulties.—If any difficulty arises in giving effect to the provisions of this Act, the State Government may, by order published in the Official Gazette, make such provisions not inconsistent with the provisions of this Act, as appear to it to be necessary or expedient for removing the difficulty:

Provided that no such order shall be made after the expiry of a period of two years from the date of the commencement of this Act.

30. Power of Central Government to give directions.—The Central Government may give directions to State Governments as to the carrying into execution of the provisions of this Act.

31. Power of Central Government to review.—The Central Government may make periodic review and monitor the progress of the implementation of the provisions of this Act by the State Governments.

32. Power of State Government to make rules.—

(*1*) The State Government may, by notification in the Official Gazette, make rules for carrying out the purposes of this Act.

(2) Without prejudice to the generality of the foregoing power, such rules may provide for—

(a) the manner of holding inquiry under section 5 subject to such rules as may be prescribed under sub-section (*1*) of section 8;

(b) the power and procedure of the Tribunal for other purposes under sub-section (*2*) of section 8;

(c) the maximum maintenance allowance which may be ordered by the Tribunal under subsection (*2*) of section 9;

(d) the scheme for management of old age homes, including the standards and various types of services to be provided by them which are necessary for medical care and means of entertainment to the inhabitants of such homes under sub-section (*2*) of section 19;

(e) the powers and duties of the authorities for implementing the provisions of this Act, under sub-section (*1*) of section 22;

(f) a comprehensive action plan for providing protection of life and property of senior citizens under sub-section (*2*) of section 22;

(g) any other matter which is to be, or may be, prescribed.

(3) Every rule made under this Act shall be laid, as soon as may be after it is made, before each House of State Legislature, where it consists of

two Houses or where such legislature consists of one House, before that House.

Chapter 6 : Old Age Homes

**Why are Old Age Homes called Old?
They are not really old. Most are far
younger than their youngest inmate.**

Old Age Homes

In India, like in most eastern countries, the traditional joint family system took care of every member of the joint family - the young, the old, the sick, the invalid, widows and widowers. There was no need of old age homes.

But all over the world, the percentage of older persons is rapidly increasing. The United Nations has classified India as an ageing country. As of July 1, 2022, India's population aged 60 and above was 149 million, which is about 10.5% of the country's population. This is projected to double to 20.8% by 2050.

The following is the statistical data relating to India's elderly population:
- 1961: 5.6%
- 2011: 8.6%
- 2021: 10.1%
- 2031: 13.1%
- 2046: Will surpass the population of children (0 to 15 years old)

But over the years, times have gradually changed. The younger generations tend to move to larger cities; to foreign countries; or otherwise separate from their parents. Some of the older people move over to the new destinations. But some can not, or do not, move over. Of course, even after migration, some persons in the younger generations continue to support their parents and relatives.

As a result, some of the older people are suddenly left with little or no physical and/or financial support. They find it difficult to adjust to the sudden financial and emotional vacuum created by the migration. A few philanthropic and charitable organizations have tried to fill up the vacuum. They have set up old age homes.

I visited a very well-established and organized old age home in Chennai (Tamil Nadu) in the late 1980s. It had large grounds and well-maintained gardens for walking around and other activities. Rooms for couples. Small cottages for couples. Pooja room. Library and common dining halls. It is always safe for two old people to stay together. It gives them companionship and immediate help, if there is any emergency.

The facilities were simple but quite satisfactory. And the charges quite nominal. I met a boy and his wife who had put their parents in this old age home because both of them were employed. They used to visit their parents every Sunday and holidays.

I talked to some of the inmates. Some had children living abroad. Some had no children. They were quite happy. The old age home provided them social security, companionship, and medical facilities. Some charitable organizations have set up old age homes. These are either free or highly subsidized. Therefore, the facilities are simple and spartan.

Over the years, there has been an increasing demand for old age homes. Several real estate developers have entered the field. They plan small conglomerations, keeping in mind the special requirements of old and retired people.

You can find a list of old homes and related matters at the following site:

https://pensionersportal.gov.in/SeniorCitizenCorner.aspx#OldAgeHomes
Open the site and click on "Old Age Homes"

HelpAge International – the oldest network for older people

HelpAge International is a global network helping older people claim their rights, challenge discrimination and overcome poverty to help them lead dignified, secure, active and healthy lives. The HelpAge International network was established in 1983 by five agencies in Canada, Colombia, India, Kenya and the UK.
The HelpAge International network has 170 members in 90 countries. The HelpAge network links more than 80 affiliates across all continents, helping to share experiences and influence national and international policies. HelpAge International also works with 180 other partners - including community organizations, NGOs, academic institutions and governments - to develop programmes and influence policy even further.

HelpAge International's work in over 90 countries is further strengthened through its global network of like-minded organizations – the only one of its kind in the world.

HelpAge India

In the late 1960s, the then speaker of the Lok Sabha visited his counterpart in the House of Commons (UK), who was also the honorary secretary of an organization called Help The Aged. Our speaker came back with the vision of setting up something similar in India. But it took 7 years for his vision to take shape. In March 1974, Mr. Jackson Cole, founder of HelpAge International, visited India. A philanthropist approached him for financial help to set up a member organization in Delhi.

Mr. Jackson Cole instead offered to train him how to raise funds. After a three-month training course in London, Samson Daniel and his wife returned to India and organized a sponsored walk with school children in Delhi. He raised sufficient funds to start a centre in Delhi. HelpAge India was registered in Delhi in April 1978. Within three months, it became autonomous as financial support from the U.K. ceased.

The present position of Old Age Homes in India

At present, there are 728 old age homes in India. Detailed information of 547 homes is available. Out of these, 325 homes are free of charge, whereas 95 homes are on pay and stay basis. 116 homes have both paid and free facilities.

A total of 278 homes are available for senior citizens, who are suffering from various types of health problems and illnesses. 101 homes are meant exclusively for women. Kerala has 124 homes – the maximum in any state.

With the steady increase in the life expectancy of individuals, there will be increasing demand for old age homes. But the requirements for senior citizens are more and have to be taken care of by the promoters and managers. I am listing some of the major requirements.

Providing Medical and Health Care Facilities

Senior citizens usually have a number of health problems and illnesses. Moreover, they have psychological problems, such as anger, stress, anxiety, frustration and depression.

Many senior citizens need medical and health care facilities regularly. Old age homes should have medical practitioners and health care specialists available regularly. There should be suitable arrangements to take sick persons to doctors and hospitals.

Providing Counselling and Guidance Services

Senior citizens also suffer from psychological problems, loneliness, seclusion, and so forth. Sometimes, purely imaginary. They need proper counselling and guidance to cope with these problems. Therefore, these old age homes should have understanding and compassionate counsellors and guidance services.

Managing Resources satisfactorily

The individuals in charge of these old age homes should be capable of efficiently managing money and resources, which are always scarce, in a satisfactory manner.

Grievance Redressal

The individuals in charge should understand that they are dealing with a different class of people. They should talk with the inmates, listen to them and try to resolve their problems – even if they are very small.

Conclusion

Old age homes enable senior citizens to live their lives with dignity and security. Measures have to be taken to enhance their numbers. And for this, Government support is necessary.

These old age homes should promote the enrichment of the status of senior citizens so that they can remain content and happy.

Chapter 7 : Retiring Early

*The challenge of retirement is how to
spend time without spending money.*

~Author Unknown

Retiring Early

Traditionally, most people worked till death, or till they became physically incapable of working any longer. The concept of retirement at a particular age is relatively new. It was introduced by Otto von Bismarck, the "Iron Chancellor" of Germany in 1889. Otto von Bismarck introduced the world's first social security scheme to attract the German working class and counter the power of the Socialist Party in Germany. It was more a political move.

Today, most developed countries have some sort of retirement age. This means that the government, or the employer, pays retirement benefits. But there are a few employees who look forward to early retirement. Some as early as 20 to 25 years before their normal retirement.

Reasons for retiring early

To find out the answer directly from the horses' mouths, I asked the children of some of my friends and colleagues, who wanted to opt for early retirement, their reasons for early retirement. The reasons were different.

Some told me that while in active service, they did not have adequate time to do all they wanted to do. Like travelling around the world. Gardening or taking care of their grandchildren. Taking an early retirement would give them the time and opportunity to do all these things which they could not do while working. Some were bored by the monotony of life. Home. Office. Back home. Meeting the same set of people day in and day out.

Advantages and Disadvantages of Early Retirement

Early retirement has both advantages and disadvantages. Both should be carefully considered. Reconsidered. And again reconsidered.

First the Disadvantages

Retiring several years before the usual retirement age has its own set of problems.
First is finance – money. Loss of a regular source of income to meet the day to day expenses and emergencies.
The second is health care.
The third is accommodation.
The fourth is loss of companionship.

A person opting for early retirement has to plan for all these. As you grow older, you may not have the strength, the interest, or the finances to do what you might have wanted to do. You will regret the days when you used to go to work, meet your co-workers, and feel you were useful and could make a difference. The tiredness at the end of a workday doesn't seem so awful now, when you have nothing to do. You will find few people to talk to and even fewer subjects to talk about.

Now the Advantages

Some senior executives will answer that they would like to get rid of their chains and lead a rather free life.

Free life would probably mean going to the gym for an hour or two. Doing some gardening or engaging in some other hobby.

Watching TV, reading newspapers, or watching a movie. Visiting friends and relatives.

And of course, travelling to different places.

The advantages of early retirement extend beyond having more time, reduced stress and independence. Early retirement - retiring before the full retirement age (usually 60 to 65) – does have specific advantages that should form part of your decision to retire early.

Retiring early does not mean total retirement. It does not mean a complete cessation of work. You can take up part-time work of the same nature you were doing earlier. You can work with NGOs. You can take up teaching. And you can time your work according to your convenience.

So should you take an early retirement?

This is a very serious decision that only you can take. The age of retirement in Canada is 65, yet just 6% of the people over 65 continue to work; generally, the real retirement age is 62. In fact, more people get out than get into the employment system. There are companies that have "retirees on call," which means that some of their former employees can be called at work part-time or when necessary, as stated in a CBC News study.

That seems to be a fair solution, both for the companies which can have the job done properly when they need, and the retirees who want an active social life and some money in addition to the benefits they are entitled to receive from the government.

Some people continue to work after formal retirement even though they get pensionery benefits. The reason is not shortage of money alone. They find retired life boring. And take up work……..may be for lesser time and with lesser pay …just to keep themselves occupied.

Professional Advice

As retirement approaches, whether it is normal or premature, it is natural to feel overwhelmed by the multitude of decisions that have to be taken. Should you shift to a smaller home? How much money you will need for your regular expenses? What will you do in case of an emergency? What steps will you take to ensure your health and well-being in your golden years if you fall sick? These are just a few of the questions that may be swirling around in your mind.

In times like these, professional advice can be a game-changer. Financial and Healthcare professionals have the knowledge and expertise to guide you through the complexities of retirement planning, ensuring that you make the best choices for your unique circumstances. While it may be tempting to rely solely on your own judgment or the advice of well-meaning friends and family, the value of personalized guidance from professionals cannot be overstated.

Unless you are very wealthy and have enough money and good accommodation, you must consult financial and healthcare professionals. They can provide you personalized guidance, helping you navigate the complexities of retirement planning and ensuring that you make the best choices for your future. After all, retirement is supposed to be a time of relaxation and enjoyment, not stress and uncertainty.

ICICI Prudential, HDFC Life, Tata AIG and similar companies have professional advisors. They will send their experts on call without any charges.

What to Expect From a Retirement Advisor

The first thing you should expect from a retirement advisor is he should have a detailed look at your complete financial picture, based on the information you provide. What are your assets? Do you have investments, real estate, pending inheritances, or other resources of value? What are your debts? Do you have a mortgage, car payments, credit cards, student loans, small business liabilities, or other loans?

How do you balance servicing your debt while still saving for retirement? What are your expenses?

Once a retirement advisor has all of your information, he will usually draft a report, providing you with a detailed financial plan for your retirement. The report will likely indicate how much money you'll be able to withdraw from your accounts each month during retirement, based on various scenarios, and how much you will need to save on a monthly basis from now until then to reach your goals. Your retirement advisor should also take into consideration the tax benefits in different schemes. Of course, he will formulate different options. You must also plan for your health care. Probably take medical insurance.

I have written two separate chapters relating to issues relating to Finance and Health which must be seriously considered before early retirement. If you take those factors into account, I assure you the transition to retirement will be smooth and stress-free.

And you will be grateful to me…

Chapter 8 : Financial Planning

**The question isn't at what age I want to retire,
it's at what income.**
George Foreman

Financial Planning

Retirement is a phase of life many of us look forward to. It's a time to relax, pursue hobbies, and enjoy the fruits of our labour. If you had unlimited funds, there would be no need for any financial planning. Unfortunately, most of us have limited resources. Therefore, in order to truly enjoy retirement, without any worries, it is important to have a solid financial plan in place. That's where creating a retirement budget comes in.

Creating a Retirement Budget

Start financial planning a few months before the planned retirement. There is no hurry. Take your time.

First and foremost, calculate your income from all sources during retirement. This may include pensions, social security and any other retirement accounts you've been diligently saving in. Take stock of all these sources and calculate how much you can expect to receive each month. It's always better to be conservative in your estimates.

Once you have a clear understanding of your income, it is time to calculate your expenses. Start by listing all your regular monthly expenses - such as housing, utilities, groceries, club bills, etc. Be sure to include any debts you may still be paying off, like a home loan or car loan. It's important to have a realistic view of your current expenses in order to plan for the future. Next, consider any additional expenses that may arise during retirement. This could include increased healthcare costs, more travel expenses, or even funding your hobbies.

It's important to factor in these extra expenses to ensure you're not caught off guard.

Now comes the fun part - make adjustments to your budget! Look for areas where you can cut back on expenses without sacrificing your quality of life. Maybe you can reduce dining out and have more meals at home. Or perhaps you can downsize your living arrangements to save on housing costs. Get creative and find ways to make your money stretch further.

Remember, a retirement budget is not set in stone. It is a living document that will have to be adjusted as your circumstances change. Stay vigilant and review your budget periodically to ensure you're on track. Always provide for a little extra for emergencies.

Investment Strategies

Creating a retirement budget is a crucial step toward financial stability during retirement. By taking the time to assess your income and expenses, and making adjustments as needed, you will be able to ensure a comfortable and worry-free retirement. So go ahead, start crunching those numbers and pave your way to a financially secure future. That's where investment strategies come into play. How to invest your money. Explore different investment options. Aim not only to protect them from the volatility of the market, but to grow your retirement funds.

One of the most popular investment options is the share market. Invest in a mix of mutual funds. There are risks involved. But with careful research and a diversified portfolio, you can minimize those risks and maximize your returns.

If you're looking for something a little less risky, you can also invest in bonds. Bonds are essentially loans given to corporations or governments. In return, you will receive regular interest payments. Bonds may give a little less returns, but they are considered less risky than shares and can provide a stable source of income during your retirement years.

Another option worth exploring is real estate. They say that investing in property is as safe as buying a house, and for good reason. Buying properties can provide a steady income stream through rental payments and the value of your property usually appreciates over time.

Spread your investments across different asset classes, such as shares, bonds, and real estate. This way, you can reduce the impact of any single investment's performance on your overall portfolio. This helps protect your retirement funds from the ups and downs of the market.

Financial Advisors

Take the help of financial advisers. They will help you create a customized investment plan based on your income and expenses, risk tolerance, goals, and time horizon. But remember, investing is not just about numbers and spreadsheets. It's also about understanding your own emotions and behavioural biases. As humans, we have a tendency to panic when the market takes a dip or to become overly confident when it's soaring. That's why it is important to stay disciplined and stick to your investment plan, even when the temptation to deviate is strong.

Whether you choose shares, bonds, real estate, or a combination all of them, the key is to approach investing with a mix of prudence and optimism. In many cases, the retirees are also entitled to Pension and Social Security benefits to some extent.

Pension Plans

Let us start with pension plans. What exactly is a pension plan? Think of a pension plan as a savings account specifically designed for retirement. Throughout your working years, a portion of your salary is set aside and invested by your employer. This money grows over time, allowing you to receive a regular income stream after your retirement. It's like having a secret stash of cash that magically appears every month to support your golden years. However, all employers do not have pension plans. In India, it is limited to the Government and the organized sector.

Social Security benefits

Well, under social benefit schemes, throughout your working years, you contribute a portion of your income to the Social Security fund. When you reach the age of retirement, the government pays you a monthly benefit based on your past earnings.

Social Security can usually just keep you going. Social Security benefits are adjusted annually to keep up with inflation, so you won't be left feeling like you're stuck in a time warp where prices never change.

Pension plans and Social Security benefits can be your best friends when it comes to retirement income. They provide a steady and assured stream of cash flow you can rely on, even when life throws curveballs your way.

Pension plans and Social Security benefits alone may not be enough to sustain your desired lifestyle in retirement. They're like the bread and butter of your financial plan – necessary, but not sufficient. That's where additional savings and investments come into play.

Tips for effectively managing debt before and during retirement

Retirement is a time for relaxation, enjoying the fruits of your labour, and finally having the freedom to pursue your passions. However, for many individuals, retirement can also carry a burden of debt.

It is essential to tackle this issue head-on and take proactive steps to manage and reduce your debt before and during retirement.

Tips for Financial Planning

I will recapitulate some valuable tips that can help you navigate the sometimes treacherous waters of debt management.
1. Create a comprehensive budget.

2. Prioritize repayment of high-interest debt.
3. Consider debt consolidation or refinancing at a lower interest rate.
4. Plan for incapacity or disablement.
5. Take professional help.
6. Decide what you want to do with your assets after death.

Estate Planning

Estate planning means making preparations for the distribution of your wealth after you are gone. You can decide to whom, which asset would pass. You can ensure a smooth transfer of your assets to your loved ones. This will avoid litigation among your heirs. The simplest solution is to make a will. I have written about this in my chapter on Wills. You will be able to prepare your own will.

Conclusion

While preparing the budget, it is always prudent to have margins for emergencies, etc. But remember, that even after retirement, you can take up some work which will fetch some income.

Chapter 9 : Health Planning

*As we grow older, we realize that
Health is as important as Wealth*

Binoy Gupta

Health Planning

We have already explored Financial Planning. Now we have to consider Planning for good Health.

Strategies for maintaining good health

As you embark on your journey towards retirement, it is crucial to prioritize your health and well-being. What good is all the free time and money if you don't have the energy and vitality to enjoy it? In this chapter, we will explore strategies to keep your body strong, your mind sharp, and your spirits vibrant.

Let us start with the physical aspect of ageing. Bodies age with time. As we grow older, we will have to take proactive steps to maintain our physical well-being. You will have to adopt a lifestyle that supports healthy ageing - which means regular exercise, a balanced diet, and sufficient rest.

Exercise

Exercise doesn't have to be a bore. Think of it as a way to stay fit, flexible, and fabulous. Onlookers should look at you and say, "See how well he has maintained himself." Do whatever suits you. A leisurely stroll in the park. Running. Jogging. Join yoga classes or a gymnasium. Or even dance like mad in the comfort of your own living room. I have several gym machines in one of my rooms. I walk on the treadmill twice a day for 30 minutes each (total 60 minutes.). That is sufficient for me.

Diet

You must have a well-balanced and nutritious diet. No. I'm not suggesting you give up all your guilty pleasures and live as if you were on a crash diet. Life is too short for tasteless meals! Instead, focus on incorporating a variety of colourful fruits and vegetables, lean proteins and whole grains. Add the occasional treat to your diet. But remember, moderation is the key. Anything in excess can only be harmful.

Rest

As we age, sleeping time gets reduced. But our bodies may need a little extra downtime to recover and recharge. So, go ahead and indulge in those midday naps guilt-free. You've earned it! And don't forget the importance of a good night's sleep. Invest in a comfortable mattress. Create a relaxing bedtime routine and banish those electronics from the bedroom. Your body and mind will thank you. (Though I am giving this advice, I have a TV in my bedroom and I watch some light serials for 30 minutes or so before sleeping.) I mean, do whatever suits you best.

Mental and Psychological Health

Good Health is not about physical health alone. It's also about the mental and psychological nurturing of our minds and spirits. Engaging in activities that challenge our brains, such as puzzles, reading, or learning a new skill, helps keep our cognitive abilities sharp.

One of the key psychological challenges that retirees often face is a sense of loss or identity crisis. For years, individuals have defined themselves through their careers. When that chapter of their lives comes to an end, they may struggle to find a new sense of purpose and meaning. This can lead to feelings of emptiness, boredom and even depression. It is therefore essential for retirees to proactively explore new interests and hobbies and engage in activities that bring them joy and fulfillment.

Many retirees find themselves with more free time, which can be both a blessing and a challenge. Without the routine of work and the camaraderie of colleagues, retirees may feel a sense of loneliness or isolation. It is important to actively seek out social interactions and build meaningful relationships with friends, family, and the community. Make new friends. Join clubs. Volunteer, or participate in group activities. These can provide you with a sense of belonging and purpose.

In addition to these practical strategies, it is also essential to prioritize self-care and mental well-being. Engage in relaxation techniques such as meditation or yoga, practice mindfulness, and seek support from therapists or support groups. All this will contribute to a positive mental state. Take the time to reflect, celebrate achievements and set new goals. This will help retirees maintain a sense of direction and purpose.

In addressing the psychological aspects of retirement and promoting mental well-being, it is important to approach the topic with a sense of humour. Retirement is a time to embrace the lighter side of life and find joy in the simple pleasures. As the saying goes, "Retirement is wonderful. It's doing nothing without worrying about getting caught."

Relationships and Social Connections

And let us not forget the power and necessity of social connections. Retirement is often seen as a time of freedom and relaxation, a chance to escape the daily grind of work and enjoy the fruits of one's labour. However, while retirement can indeed be a wonderful phase of life, it also brings with it a set of challenges, particularly when it comes to personal relationships. The transition from a structured work environment to an unstructured retirement lifestyle can have a significant impact on relationships, including friendships and family relationships.

In the workplace, we often form strong bonds with colleagues, sharing experiences, and relying on each other for support. When retirement comes, these connections suddenly fade away, leaving retirees feeling isolated and lonely. Suddenly, old friends and colleagues disappear.

To maintain healthy connections outside of the workplace, retirees must actively work on building and nurturing friendships. They will have to find new friends and acquaintances.

This may involve joining social groups or clubs, volunteering, or even reaching out to old friends and colleagues. By actively seeking out social opportunities and making an effort to stay connected, retirees can combat feelings of isolation and build a strong support network to lean on during this new chapter of their lives.

For many couples, work has been a central aspect of their lives, providing structure, routine, and a shared sense of purpose. When retirement comes, there is a shift in dynamics within their intimate relationships and couples find themselves spending much more time together.

While this may sound like a dream come true, it can also lead to tensions and conflicts. Suddenly, partners who were used to having their own space and independence find themselves in constant proximity, which can be overwhelming.

To navigate this challenge, it is important for couples to communicate openly and establish new boundaries. This may mean setting aside individual time and pursuing separate interests. It is crucial to remember that individual identities and interests are essential for a healthy relationship, even in retirement. By maintaining a sense of independence and supporting each other's personal pursuits, couples can avoid the pitfalls of excessive togetherness and foster a more balanced and fulfilling retirement.

Additionally, family dynamics can change as retirees find themselves spending more time with adult children or grandchildren. While this can be a source of joy and fulfillment, it can also bring its own set of challenges, such as navigating different expectations and boundaries.

Remember, retirement is not just about financial planning or choosing the perfect old-age home. It is about embracing the opportunities that come with this new phase of life and nurturing the relationships that matter most. So, as you embark on your retirement journey, remember to laugh, love, and stay connected.

Preventive Care and Health Screenings

Maintaining Good Health is very important. Visualize your body as a well-oiled machine. It runs smoothly, operates efficiently and keeps you going day in and day out. But remember, even the most well-maintained machines can develop problems over time. Our bodies are no exception. That's where preventive care comes in. Visit your healthcare provider regularly. This will allow them to assess your overall health and detect and treat many potential issues before they escalate into major problems.

Prevention is better than cure. Just like changing the oil in your car or getting your teeth cleaned, regular check-ups and screenings play a vital role in preventing and detecting health issues early. These routine visits to the doctor are essential for maintaining your overall well-being.

We will explore why preventive care and health screenings are so important and how they can benefit you in the long run. Preventive care doesn't just focus on identifying existing health issues. It's also about keeping you in the best possible shape to prevent future problems. During your check-ups, your doctor will assess various aspects of your health, such as your blood pressure, cholesterol levels, and body mass index. They will provide guidance on healthy lifestyle choices, offer recommendations for vaccines, and discuss any screenings or tests that may be relevant for you based on your age, gender, and medical history.

Speaking of screenings, let's talk about them for a moment. These are specialized tests designed to identify specific health conditions early.

From mammograms to colonoscopies, these screenings are like Sherlock Holmes, searching for any signs of trouble within your body. They can detect cancer, heart disease, diabetes, and a whole host of other conditions that might be silently developing within you. So, even if you're feeling fine, don't shy away from these tests. They might help detect serious diseases early. They might even save your life!

Don't underestimate the power and benefits of preventive care and health screenings. Don't skip these because you feel fit and fine. They are undoubtedly essential for maintaining your health and well-being. Make it a priority to schedule those check-ups, embrace those screenings and take control of your health as advised by your doctors.

After all, retirement is all about enjoying life to the fullest. And what better way to do that than by investing in your own health? Stay healthy, stay happy, and keep those awkward screening stories coming! And remember, retirement is not the end of the road. It is the beginning of a new and exciting chapter. Learn to enjoy every single moment. And if all else fails, remember this joke to lighten the mood: Why did the retired couple go on a cruise? Because they wanted to sail away from all their worries and enjoy some well-deserved relaxation in the sun!

Chapter 10 : From my Personal Experiences

You can and should enjoy your life after retirement provided you had planned your future in advance.

This Book will teach you all that you need to know.

From my Personal Experiences

I will share my personal experiences with you. After 37 years of service, I retired from Government Service on 30 September 2005. It is an irony in superior Government services that officers reach the top most positions at the fag end of their career, that is, just before retirement. I was on top of Mount Everest till 30 September 2005. The next day, I was nobody. It was a very steep fall.

After that, I have enjoyed retired life for more than 18 years. There are problems specific to retirement. But proper understanding, psychological preparedness and making proper arrangements, made the journey smooth.

Some retirees do not have children, or their children do not look after them. What should they do? Old Age Homes are a practical solution. I have given details of Old Age Homes.

Sometimes, there are quarrels and litigation after the death of the retiree. Children and relatives fight like cats and dogs. Litigation in courts in India drag on for decades. Preparing a will is a simple and practical solution. I have written a full chapter on Wills. You can prepare your will yourself.

The main problems after retirement are Finance and Health. I have dealt exhaustively with how to prepare for both.

This book contains a wealth of information for those due for retirement and for those who want to opt for early retirement. After all, a person wants to be happy and enjoy life after retirement. Free of tensions. This is the master key.

After my retirement, we went on a Princess cruise from US to Alaska. We simply enjoyed the 10 days. The ship had a heated swimming pool, a gymnasium on the top, unlimited food, medical attendants and mini theatre halls. There were a lot of senior citizens on board.

We have followed all the rules discussed in this book and are quite content and happy.

About the Author

Dr. Binoy Gupta

The author retired as a top bureaucrat in the Government of India. He holds a Ph.D. in law as well as a large number of post graduate degrees and diplomas. He has authored several books and written hundreds of articles. He was a regular commentator on Radio and T.V. He was guest faculty member of the Department of Management Studies in Madras University.

He has interacted with a large number of people and seen the problems faced by retired people. Most of these problems can be resolved by proper planning.

This book will tell you all about retirement. Financial and Health Planning. Wills. Old Homes.

And help you attain a comfortable, Wealthy and Healthy life.